£1·00

Straight from the Heart
by
Mike Bowen

THE MEETING ROOM
BOOK AND COFFEE SHOP
BEDFORD ROW, TEMPLE BAR.
½PRICE EXCHANGE. PH: 6266982
OPEN SEVEN DAYS A WEEK.

Published by:
M.J. BOWEN PTY. LTD.,
28 The Deviation,
Wheeler's Hill, Victoria 3150.

Illustrated by:
RACHEL HUELESBUSCH
31 Gracedale Ave,
Bayswater Nth., Victoria.

Photos by:
JOHN N. ROSE.
51 Dandelion Drive,
Rowville, Victoria 3178

Cover by:
MARIUS FOLEY

Typesetting by:
WITCHTYPE PTY LTD
11/37 Albert Road,
Melbourne, Victoria 3004

Printed by:
THE CRAFTSMAN PRESS PTY. LTD.
125 Highbury Road,
Burwood, Victoria 3125.

© M.J. BOWEN 1989

Contents

Come on in	1	Fantasy Amber	24
Reflections	2	Birthmark	25
My Beloved Co Kerry (in Ireland)	3	If Dreams Came True	26
Making a Mistake	4	This World's For All	27
My Love Poem	5	The Professional	28
The Divorce I	6	Pollution	29
The Divorce II	6	1962	30
I Never Knew Him	7	Autumn Leaves	31
Trees	8	Stay With Me	32
Hunger Strike	9	Monday Faces	33
Skateboard	10	Once In A Lifetime	34
Dublin	11	Your My Everything	35
Deceiving Me	12	Wattle Tree Park	36
Vietnam	13	Life is Tough	38
Arc de Triomphe September 1988	14	Drugs	39
16 in 1916	15	Soccer	40
The Hobo	16	Eyes of Fire	41
To My Mum Liz With Love	17	T.V.	42
My Nan Liz	17	Bombay	43
Michael K	18	Loving You	44
Headlines	19	Losing You	45
40	20	Men's Perms	46
Seasons of Love	21	What Would You Say	47
Losing Dad	22	What Do We Really See	48
Poets World	23	Freedom Come	49

Acknowledgements

The very young and talented Rachel Huelsebusch for her illustrations.
John Noel Rose, for his time and patience in photographing me. A true professional.
George Wilson for all his help.
To Joe Magill
The A.M.P Society
To Michael Kavanagh for his inspiration.
To my family.
To Ireland for giving me the strength.
To Australia for giving me the opportunity.

Foreword

What is it, that intangible quality that transforms adversity and deprivation into glorious success?

Is it a spark of genius that is spawned from the fires of tough times, or is it just sheer determination?

Mike left school in his native Ireland, an illiterate at age thirteen, but he has risen above this lack of formal education to give the world such beautifully styled and feeling poems as in this book.

Mike loves to write from his own experiences but his love and caring for his fellow man has brought poems on topics as diverse as the St Kilda kids and the purveyors of destruction like French boat bombing terrorists.

Mike has taken a lot of flak over the years with his "Poet with a car-phone" tag. But once again there lies a story of Mike's determination to succeed. He sent a copy of his first collection of poems "Window to my soul" to the "Age" for review and wouldn't take "No" for an answer. He was arguing the toss with the literary editor who steadfastly refused to mention the book until the conversation got round to where Mike was ringing from.

The stunned Editor gave him a review ... incredulous that a poet should have a car phone. He needs one of course, as a retirement counsellor with the AMP.

Read carefully and thoughtfully the following pages.

They represent the spark of genius.

John Reid
John Reid's Poet Corner
7.10 am Sundays, Melbourne's 3LO

Come On In

Come on in and take a look
All you want is in this book
Facts of life and some love too
I wrote this book just for you
The fantasies that you want to reach
The joy of laying on a beach
Some sadder days I will recall
I'll lift you up, not let you fall
So come on in, pull up a chair
Move in close and let's be near

Reflections

I look in my mirror
just for a while
and in my face
I see your smile
I see the future
I see the past
as I look into
my looking glass

Don't dislike me
for what I'm not
Like me for what I am

I can live with the pain
As long as the sun still shines
and it don't rain

My Beloved Co Kerry (in Ireland)

Oh Jesus, Kerry I love you
Because of what you make me do
I burn your light deep inside
Emotions now I cannot hide
You make my blood run so fast
The joys we shared in the past
I love you like a virgin bride
Your people show me so much pride
Oh Kerry make me part of you
There's nothing I would rather do
To spend my days here with you
Would make my greatest wish come true

Making a mistake

*Of all the experiences
that I've ever had
the one that really
hurts so bad
is to love someone
and know it's right
then keep it shaded
from the light*

*If you love someone
please let them know
for I know you'll
regret it when they go
love with a passion
there's no other way
don't put it off
'til another day*

*Kiss her right now
not a moment too late
before she packs and
walks out the gate*

My Love Poem

I'm writing a love poem for you
Cos baby I love all you do
You make me feel good
Just the way I should
So I'm writing a love poem for you

I love you for always
For ever and a day
I'll love you for ever
In my special way

There's no other way I could say
Those things to you
But darling you know
All I say is true

Won't you come and lie beside me
Let me feel you hold me tight
Baby don't you leave me
In the dark of night

I've written this love poem for you
Cos baby I love all you do
I want you for always
For ever and a day
I'll love you for ever
In a very special way

The Divorce I

I had an awful shock today
My son who is so far away
Was in an accident and nearly died
The tears just poured, Oh how I cried
I left our home some years ago
To return again, I did not know
13 years has passed, I miss him so
I don't think he will every really know
What it was like to say goodbye
The years just went so swiftly by
I wish I could tell him how I feel
Though he may think it is no big deal
A father's love does not just die
Sometimes the only thing he can do is cry

The Divorce II

There's a girl I love, and she'll never know
Because I wasn't there to see her grow
She was only one, when we said goodbye
And she won't let me tell her why
I want her to know she's part of me
I just want to make her see
What went wrong and what makes me sad
Whether she likes it or not, I'm still her dad

I Never Knew Him

*I never really knew him
And I guess I never will
Although I always loved him
And I love him still*

*I'm mad at him for what he's done
To keep us both apart
Although I dearly love him
Although we're miles apart*

*We never said hello
And we never said goodbye
For in my heart all those years
I've always wondered why*

*He never really spoke to me
I guess that was his way
He never ever squeezed my hand
But I wish he would today*

*A father's got to know his son
It's the way it must be
What's the point in having kids
What's the point in me?*

*You know I idolised him
From the moment I could see
But all the time he looked
And never looked at me*

Trees

It's strange the way you look at me
Just because I'm a tree
Do you realise that I'm real
Can you believe that I can feel
I get sick just like you
Except there's nothing I can do
But you can help me to grow tall
Please don't chop me, I'll just fall
I can help you when I grow
I'll give you shelter from the snow
And when the sun begins to shine
You can lay your body next to mine

Hunger Strike

When my stomach aches beyond belief
And no movement gives me relief
I start to wonder if it's worthwhile
Then I bear it with a smile

It's the ultimate sacrifice I can make
To give my life for your sake
So treasure this country when I'm dead
And lay these words at my head

Bobby Sands was my name
England again was to blame
Another murder for the Crown
I never let my country down

Skateboard

*Flying along like a bird on the wing
Then I felt it o' that awful sting
I must have fallen so many times
I'm beginning to hear permanent chimes
Skateboards are for little children
Definitely not for dads and mums
If I lose any more teeth
I will only have gums*

Dublin

I remember autumn in Dublin
and how it melted my heart
I remember so much about Dublin
I really don't know where to start
A grey autumn night at The Peacock
The warmth of her hand in mine
As we walked down O'Connell Street together
To look for some place where to dine
A stroll in the green on Fridays
Just to watch the world go by
I thought I must be in heaven
But I just couldn't understand why
The feeling of warmth in The Merchant
We sang till our hearts were content
The band sang a song for Ireland
As I wondered what it all meant
There is so much gaiety in Dublin
That it really is hard to describe
This feelin' of love from the Irish
It is something that you feel inside
I hope when I die there's a Dublin
A tranquil place for you and I
A place where all can be happy
Somewhere up in the sky

Deceiving Me

You said that you loved me
when we first met
you said when we were married
I would never regret

We had just settled down
in our new little home
when you started your excuses
you couldn't reach a phone

I turned a blind eye
to all that you'd done
do I still love you
it was not much fun

I did all I could
though I know love fades
what I didn't know then
you were giving me AIDS

Vietnam

I was just 19, when I answered the call
Thought I would join up and have me a ball
I'd go to Vietnam to fight for their rights
But I wasn't prepared for those Vietnam sights
If I sat down and wrote for a hundred years
There is no way I could describe this valley of tears
It was such a puzzle it was such a maze
It was virtually impossible to see through the haze
Now I live alone in this thin little shed
And I re-run the war in my confused head
My family left me a long time ago
Said they didn't really want to know
My mates call to see me to check if I'm right
They know what I've got to cope with at night
You'd really have had to be there, to know what I mean
O God how I wish I never had been
Maybe one day politicians will get their act right
And poor bastards like me won't have to fight

Arc de Triomphe September 1988

As I stood there and cried
For all those who died
I remember the hell
Please let me tell
How we shared with the rats
And dined on our cats
How we lay in the mud
As our friends poured with blood
War is not sweet, when there's nothing to eat
The glory is lost, as you lie in the frost
So when you're taking the picture
Of the monument so fair
Please give some thought
For those who died here

16 in 1916

He said how do I look
She said you look fine
You're the best looking soldier
And I'm glad you're mine

"I'm off to the war"
He said with a smile
I will only be gone
For a very short while

He was only sixteen
And not yet a man
But off he did go
To do what he can

Sixteen's much too young
To be fighting a war
When you don't even know
What you are fighting for

As war holds no luck
For young and for old
He soon would be lying
Stone dead and quite cold

The fine glory of war
Is so misunderstood
I'd outlaw the game
If only I could

The Hobo

I put his food out every night
I watch him eat it with delight
The lonely hobo who walks the street
With battered shoes upon his feet

I wonder why God put him here
When no-one seems to give a care
I watch him stumble from my door
And wonder if he'll be back once more

To my Mum Liz with love

Liz, my Mum whom I adore
shall live in my heart for evermore
Her loving ways, and gentle smile
for her I'd walk many a mile
When I was small, life was tough
and with my Mum, Dad was rough
She took life's knocks on the chin
and bore it all with a grin
She prayed and prayed every day
and never really had a say
Lord when you take her away from me
won't you help me to see
Where she was right and I was wrong
Lord won't you help me to be strong?

My Nan Liz

The sweetest lady that I ever knew
Was the one who watched me as I grew
She was a glowing shining light
She kept me safe from the night
I watched, and learned all I could
All she gave was so good
I listened to every word she said
Sadly now, my Nan is dead
I loved her dearly till the end
I always saw her as my friend

Michael K.

Mike, my friend whom you all know
Nearly died two years ago
He's buzzing around like a bee
Says he's going to outlive me
He's looking good and feeling great
He only looks twenty eight
Says he's grateful for his life
So agrees his child and wife
The guts he's got I've never known
But in his trouble, they were shown
Fought his fight, and how he won
Now his fighting days are done
Says he's back to needle me
Gee it is so good to see
To all of you who are suffering pain
At times it's driving you insane
Think of Mike my closest friend
Who's really on the road to mend

Headlines

So you want to be a pop star
You want the glory and the fame
To buy the morning tabloids
Just to see your name

You want the chauffeur-driven car
The champagne and the fun
You want to win the marathon
But you just don't want to run

Well just remember getting there
Isn't all lights and cheer
For those on top have worked non-stop
And that's what got them there

40

Now I have reached 40, I am over the moon
I know you will be 40 too, real soon
There is nothing to fear, now that I am there
I wonder why I worried all of last year
Was I scared to grow up, just like Dad
When I look back now, I feel so sad
Life is all about giving not of your age
I'm sure glad that I, have reached this stage
For when you reach 40 you are in your prime
I don't know about you but I am in mine

Seasons of Love

Walk with me, in the springtime of my life
Smile for me in the sad times of my life
Bathe with me in the summers of my life
Care for me in the lost times of my life
Wrap around me in the autumn of my life
Bare with me in the troubled times of my life
Love me in the winter of my life
And I will love you, for all of my life

Losing Dad

I'm scared of grog I know I am
Because of what Dad did to Mam
It made our lives a living hell
I'm glad that I can write to tell
The T.V. makes it look so nice
It doesn't tell you of the vice
My Dad got hooked when he was young
And like a bee it stung and stung
It's sad to see him fade away
I watch him drink every day
He's lost control he cannot stop
Now I know I've lost my Pop
Do we young kids have to carry the shame
Will breweries and governments not share the blame?

Poets World

I opt out of this world
With my paper and pen
Transcend to a place
Only a few have been

The world of poets
Such a nice place to be
With the flow of words
And my soul running free

To write all that's true
With the freedom of choice
I hope I can do it
As well as James Joyce

Fantasy Amber

Come on Fred, let's go out tonight
I'm in the mood to fly my kite
Let's go down to the pub and have us a ball
Pick up the phone and give John a call
Grab the old Kingswood and I'll grab some beer
Let's jump in the car and get out of here
Keep your eyes on the road, I hope we're not late
Jesus Fred mind that old gate
John's looking drunk, but I've had more than him
It must be after slipping him that Mickie Finn
Fred let me drive I know the way
Let's go to the disco down by the bay
That moron in front doesn't know how to drive
I'll toot the ol' bastard see if he's alive
Isn't this fun mate, I'm having a ball
O Jesus Fred we'll hit that wall

Did you know them well, the policeman said
I'm afraid lad, your mates are dead

Birthmark

Hi Dad, what's that you got?
I really thought you got shot
It's a birthmark on my bum
No son, it's not gum

Did you have a heart attack Dad?
If you had I'd be so sad
No son, I'm really okay
I'm sure I'll live another day

What's a birthmark, does it hurt?
Will it rub off on your shirt?
The doctor said it's lucky son
Though having one is not fun

Can I have one just the same?
Son, you're driving me insane
Ask your Mum if it's alright
Wouldn't you sooner have a kite?

If Dreams Came True

I had a dream that you were mine
All the world was new I was in love with you

And if dreams came true I'd be in love with you
There's nothing I couldn't do, baby if dreams came true

I'd make the stars shine bright both day and night
I'd make the moon shine too, baby just for you
I'd have a fresh wind blow where ever you'd go
I'd let the whole world know how much I love you so

I'd build a house in the sky, baby for you and I
And we could live by the sun, baby wouldn't it be fun
I'd have the seasons changed, I'd have them re-arranged
We'd have our spring in the fall, we'd have no winter at all

I'd make your wishes come true just by loving you
And we could walk hand in hand, we could make love in the sand
and we would sure have a ball, nothing would matter at all
But my dreams come true and my loving you

And if dreams came true I'd be in love with you
There's nothing I couldn't do, baby if dreams came true

This World's For All

*I just don't understand what's wrong with France today
She seems to be so keen, to blow our world away
They're fighting wars and testing bombs
and sinking peace boats too
Soon I hope you realise there are others here with you
This world's for all and not for one
We just don't want to fight
Stop your testing in our park
Let others have their right*

The Professional

I saw you begin a feeble star
I wonder what made you what you are
Was it looks that got you there
Not what I can see from here
Was it something deep inside
A thing they call professional pride

Pollution

Let's contemplate just for a while
Let's focus on our life style
Pollution poisons the air we breathe
We only ever think of greed
Open your eyes and look around
So much garbage on the ground
Plastic seems to rule the day
Big business always gets its way
Pour the oil down the sink
Kill the fish, make a stink
Chop the forest, poison the sea
Not the way it was meant to be
This world's been here for millions of years
Now it seems no one cares

1962

*Today I wandered back to 1962
I thought of all the crazy things
and how much I loved you*

*We sang songs of love and joy
with flowers in our hair
We sang songs of love and joy
love was everywhere*

*I wandered through my memories
to see what I could find
Standing there in front of me
I must have been blind*

*I saw you with eyes of blue
and your red lips on
After all those crazy years
where did we go wrong*

*Looking back I'm wiser now
but it's much too late
I don't suppose there's a chance
we could make a date?*

Autumn Leaves

Autumn leaves turning brown
Autumn leaves falling down
I love you, don't fade away
Hold my hand please won't you stay

Winter snow on the ground
Winter frost all around
I love you, don't steal away
Brighten up this winter's day

Springtime comes, brings the sun
Reminds me now when I was young
I love you, please look my way
Let's make love this springtime day

Summer smiles everywhere
Summer magic in the air
I love you, do you love me
Kiss me now for all to see

Stay With Me

All I ever want is you
girl to make my dreams come true
just to brighten up my days
show me love in so many ways
just to see your lovely smile
for to hold you all the while

O I could make the stars shine bright
and I could give you cloudless nights
I would always hold you near
you would never know of fear
and I would hold you like a dove
just for a moment of your love

I could give you everything
even make the robins sing
I could make your dreams come true
if you would only love me too
I could love you all my life
if you would only be my wife

Monday Faces

*Monday faces everywhere
Empty faces that just stare
Let me see your Friday smile
Let me hold you for a while*

*Monday faces get me down
Everywhere I see a frown
Friday seems to bring more cheer
Especially this time of year*

*Monday always seem to rain
Drowsy head and more pain
Friday never comes too fast
Then it never seems to last*

*Monday always makes me sad
Think it's time I was a dad
Going to ask her to be mine
Then Mondays will be fine*

*Monday faces everywhere
Empty faces that just stare
Let me see your Friday smile
Let me hold you for a while*

MONDAY FACE

FRIDAY SMILE

Once in a Lifetime

I'm glad I got the memory
and thrown away the dream
I wondered all those years
just how it might have been
would it be nice
would it be sweet
would it be good
enough to eat
to say it was exciting
well that wouldn't be quite true
it was so very much better
I'm glad it was with you

You're My Everything

Baby you're my heartaches
You're my hurt and pain
Baby you're my sunshine
Turned into rain

Baby you're my conscience
Window to my soul
Baby you're a heartache
Out of control

Baby you're the sorrow
Cutting deep inside
Baby you're the anguish
That I can't hide

Baby you're the teardrop
Running down my face
And you can be as
Sweet as midnight lace

Baby be my rainbow
Colouring in my days
Baby be my sunshine
In winter haze

Baby be the life light
Shining in my life
Oh baby be the one
I call my wife

Wattle Tree Park

*The Wattle Tree tram
Hasn't moved for years
It doesn't have wheels
And it doesn't have stairs
She said "Let's go in
There isn't a gate"
So in we did go
To fornicate*

Life Is Tough

So you think you've got it tough
and you just don't want to fight
come and take a walk with me
in St Kilda any night

Come on down and bring your friends
and they bring their friends too
you're in for a hell of a shock
it'll scare the pants off you

You can walk among the street kids
and watch them being abused
while the call girls eye, the pushers shy
and the pimps look on amused

You tell me that life is tough
as you look down from your ivory tower
stop whingeing and crying, get off your arse
make this your finest hour

Drugs

Speak to me of love and hope
Tell me of the kids on dope
We allow it to happen under our nose
Then we say, "Ah, that's how it goes"
You want to protect your children
Then listen to me
Open your eyes and you may see
You know what you can do to lend a hand
In this we call the Lucky Land
You can dob on pushers, and importers too
Hey, don't snub me, this can happen to you
If you love your kids, you must be strong
Stand by their sides, and they'll never go wrong

Soccer

Football is my favourite game
Ever since I was small
I'll never forget my sixth birthday
When Dad gave me a ball
I've loved the game for so many years
The highs, the lows, and through the tears
The thrills I've had when times were bad
I've never remembered feeling sad
But us fans got old and times got bold
It sure makes me think a lot
These days I'm just plain scared to go
In case that I get shot

Eyes of Fire

Eyes of fire heart of gold
Lips so sweet smile so bold
Say you love me just once more
Please don't turn to face that door

Now eyes of fire burn in my soul
Of my life I've lost control
I feel such warmth so much within
I'm sure to God it's not a sin

Eyes of fire your passion's sweet
You make my life such a treat
Say you love me all the time
Swear to God you'll be mine

Eyes of fire I can't be wrong
Do you know what's going on
I've tried to tell you all along
I thought it best I'd write a song

O eyes of fire tell me true
Do you love me as I love you
Say you love me just once more
Please don't turn to face that door

T.V.

T.V. sometimes is worse than a drug
It seems to treat you like a mug
You sit there and stare and soak it all in
It's got to be society's garbage bin
It never gives, it only takes
It thrives on all our mistakes
It says how to give, and how to buy
But it never gives, the reason why
It shows us the bad, rarely the glad
For it always seems to make us sad
It stopped the stories Dad used to tell
It sent our social life to hell

Bombay

It was the worst garbage can that I've ever seen
It's called Bombay, can you imagine what I mean
The smell of stench I can still recall
As the wealthy danced at the Ambassadors' Ball
The poor mingled with the hungry rats
As the gentry smiled and tipped their hats
The children played in the mounds of shit
And the flies didn't seem to mind one bit
We mustn't have no heart at all
To let human dignity take such a fall

Loving You

*Maybe one day I will see
what it was all meant to be
Was I supposed to run away
and worry about it another day
For who knows really what is right
and what causes us to fight
Is love blind well maybe so
but no one really seems to know
When I'm older and much more wise
it will be too late to realise*

Losing You

Talk to my best friend
and tell her how you feel
Tell her of your love for me
though it may sound unreal
Tell her how I walked away
just because I couldn't say
I love you, 'cos you are you
and we could really start anew
The past has gone forever
to be repeated never
So let's look forward
don't look behind
When I lost you
I sure was blind

Men's Perms

Hair, O dear
how silly I feel
just to have some appeal
rollers in my hair
no wonder they stare
I feel so silly
I look like Lilly
Who's that I see
Joe's looking at me
Hey I'm no pansy
I'm not your dandy
The things I go through
Just to look nice for you

What Would You Say

What would you say
O babe if I could find a way
To make all of your dreams
Come true

You'd look at me
And maybe you would see
I'm the solution to all
Of your strife

Well just you hold on
The fantasy is gone
And I don't have the
Answer to life

Everybody takes
And no one wants to give
Oh those days, that's
How we live

There is no easy way
You just work every day
And love those, who
Give and don't take

So what can I say
To take the pain away
Would it help if I
Hold you near

Well just you hold tight
And squeeze with all your might
I don't want to leave
You tonight

What Do We Really See?

As I sit in my chair
And I watch you stare
You think that I'm dead
Cos I can't move my head
You don't think I'm alive
Just because I can't jive
I see more than you
You don't have a clue
How I see my life
All you see is strife
It's not what you see
I know what I am
I'm God's special gift
To my precious Mam

Freedom Come

*Hey come on you Irish
and sing with me loud
We're an island of fighters
and that's why I'm proud*

*For the sake of our freedom
that is yet to come
Let's show them damn Brits
that we are not dumb*

*They maim and they kill
They say that it's right
Then they expect us
to watch and not fight*

*They rode on our backs
for too many years
Let's show them damn bastards
that we have no fears*

*Let's throw them damn Brits
back in to the sea
We're an island of fighters
who want to be free*

*Let's give them a fight
that we may be proud
Come sing with me Irish
and sing with me loud*

*And let's pray for the day
that our freedom comes*